I can do my measuring

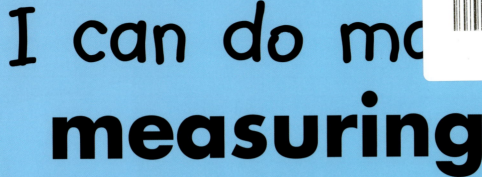

Written by Debbie Green
Illustrated by Richard Johnston

How to use this book…
1) Find the missing stickers
2) Write the answers in the spaces
3) Wipe the answers clean and try again

Which sandcastle is tallest? Which sandcastle is shortest? Add the missing flags.

Which crab looks heaviest? Which crab looks lightest? Add the missing claws.

Which bucket is the most full? Which bucket is the least full? Add the missing pictures.

Which child is building the biggest sandcastle? Find some sticker sandcastles to help.

Which flip-flop is the longest? Which flip-flop is the shortest? Find the matching flip-flops.

Which fish is the widest? Which fish is the narrowest? Find the missing tails.

Which cone will hold the most ice cream?
Which will hold the least?
Find the missing ice cream stickers.

Use the sticker rulers to find out the length of each spade. Which is the longest?

Find the missing stickers, then read the scales to find the weight of each shell.

.... g .... g .... g

Find the sticker beakers and say how much juice is in each. Which beaker is the fullest?

.... ml   .... ml   .... ml

Find the stickers and read the tickets to see which child will go on the pedal boats first. Who will go last?

Find the widest crab, the thinnest spade and the bucket that will hold the most water.

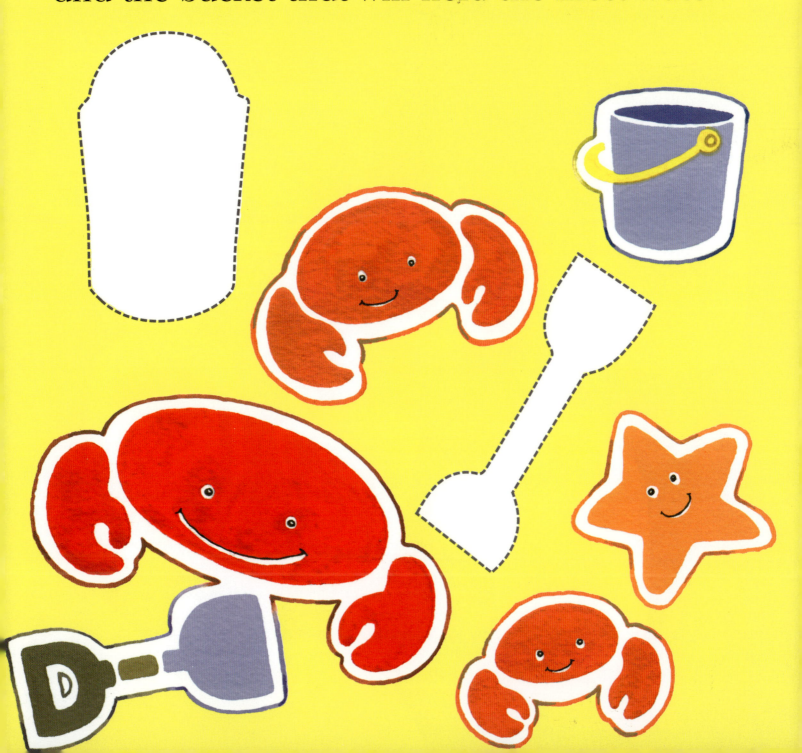

Find a squash bottle with 500ml in it, a bottle with 900ml in it and one with 1 litre in it.

Find the missing stickers, then estimate which lollipop is 6cm wide, and which is 3cm wide.

It's 4 o'clock. Dev, Dom and Heena are waiting for a bus home. Which bus will leave first? Who must wait the longest?